EL GRECO

Δομήνικος Θεοτοκόπουλος
(El Greco)

MANOLIS

libros libertad
2007

Δομήνικος Θεοτοκόπουλος εποία*
Domenikos Theotokopoulos

*English translation: "Created by Domenikos Theotokopoulos"

El Greco (Δομήνικος Θεοτοκόπουλος) (1541—April 7, 1614) was a prominent painter, sculptor and architect of the Spanish Renaissance. He always signed his paintings in Greek letters with his full name «Δομήνικος Θεοτοκόπουλος εποία.» At other times in order to signify his actual place of birth, Fodele, a village in the island of Crete, he added the word «Κρής,» (Cretan), as in «Δομήνικος Θεοτοκόπουλος, Κρής, εποία.» He traveled to Venice to study. In 1570 he moved to Rome where he opened his own workshop and executed a series of works. In 1577 El Greco emigrated to Toledo, Spain, where he lived and worked until his death.

El Greco developed into an artist so unique that he belongs to no conventional school. His dramatic and expressionistic style was met with puzzlement by his contemporaries but gained newfound appreciation in the 20th century. His is best known for tortuously elongated figures and other fantastic or phantasmagorical pigmentation, marrying Byzantine traditions with those of Western civilization. According to evidence from his time, Domenikos Theotokopoulos (El Greco) acquired his name, not only for his place of origin, but also for the sublimity of his art: "Out of the great esteem he was held in he was called the Greek (el Greco)"

First published by:
Libros Libertad Publishing Ltd.
PO Box 45089
12851 16th Avenue, Surrey, BC, V4A 9L1
Ph. (604) 838-8796
Fax (604) 536-6819
www.libroslibertad.ca

Library and Archives Cataloguing in Publication

Manolis, 1947–
    El Greco : Domenikos Theotokopoulos / Manolis.
Poems.

ISBN 978-0-9781865-4-8

    1. Greco, 1541?-1614—Poetry. I. Title.
PS8626.A673G74 2007   C811'.6   C2007-902221-9

Design and layout by Vancouver Desktop Publishing Centre
Printed in Canada by Printorium Bookworks

Praise for the Works of the Author

It's hard to write poetry of affirmation in a post-modernist culture where irony is a compulsive tic. But this new collection by Manolis, a series of meditations on the life and work of the great Cretan artist Domenikos Theotokopoulos (El Greco), triumphs in its lyric intensity and open-hearted transcendentalism. This is a celebration of Hellenic culture and an affirmation of human aspiration amid the chaos of history and the muddle of consensus reality. The poet discovers epiphanies of a heightened vision in the iconography of the paintings. The offset four-line stanza form gives space for reflection and shape to his unfolding narrative.

As the poet enters the space where El Greco worked and sits before the canvasses he's overcome by what the philosopher Colin Wilson calls "Faculty X"—an existential grasp of the actuality of the past as a living present, an intuitive *gnosis*. "The movement of the brush /waves through the air of/ sulphur and darkness." Vivid images from nature are linked with the exalted vision of the painter, creating a Blakean sense of the world as suffused with a divine energy. As we contemplate the paintings, reproduced in the book, our own vision is re-energised and refreshed.   —*Paul A. Green*

I believe that people like Conrad, Nabokov, Jonas, Manolis, and Bronowski have an advantage in crossing over from another language; they do things with English words which native speakers would never think of. El Greco illustrates my point superbly.   —*John Skapski*

I think Manolis Aligizakis is the best emigré Greek writer in Canada and I welcome his return to publishing.

—*J. Michael Yates*

The Orphans does not intend to change the world; it intends to open the people's eyes. —Now Newspaper

I'm touched by the poetry of this man . . . —*Winnie McCormick*

The Orphans definitely stirs up conversation and debate. One doesn't necessary agree with all in this book, yet a few things hit the nail on the head. —*Chuck Grodzicki*

With smooth wholeness of imagery, with lively characters and detail descriptions Manolis Aligizakis presents his new novel . . . Stratis Roukounas . . .

—*Aristidis Mavridis, editor in chief,* Literary Annual Review, *Athens, Greece, January 1982*

Sleep, dream, and ecstasy are the
three open gates to the beyond from
where come towards us the science of
the soul and the art of clairvoyance.
Evolution is the essence of life.
Number is the essence of cosmos.
Unity is the essence of God.

—*Pythagorean Initiation Psalm*

I learn in heavens means I truly see.
I learn on earth means I recall.
Blessed be the one who is initiated into
the cosmic secrets, because he truly
knows his purpose in life.

—*Pindar*

For Rocio, Larry, and Alex

Other Works by Manolis

Path of Thorns, poetry,
Libros Libertad Publishing, Vancouver, BC, 2006

Footprints in Sandstone, poetry
Authorhouse, Bloomington, Indiana, 2006

The Orphans–an Anthology, poetry
Authorhouse, Bloomington, Indiana, 2005

Stratis o Roukounas, novel, (in Greek)
Aristidis Mavridis Publishing, Athens-Greece, 1981

Spathis-322, novel (translated in English)
Condensed form published in
Canadian Fiction Magazine, Translation issue: Spring 1976

Contents

Dawn

Nauseated with the littleness
of city non-living,
the savage humdrum
mind grasping splinters

> on the surface of nowhere
> never sated with the neck-down delights
> and all carnal pleasures,
> I embark on a quest for that

special conifer, the sequoia,
that special flower in the midst
of the impassable thicket
the man who sees man as man.

> Many a time with tenderness
> I shared a soft pillow with
> a hardened, suspicious Death.
> Many a time I took Him

by the hand when He felt left
behind, when He felt abandoned.
In the noise of the marketplace
I glanced at Him. He smiled at me. Usually.

I dared Him to a jog once,
perhaps twice, and,
with a sardonic laugh, He declined.
With His perennial laughter

He shares with me a non-fat latte
at the neighborhood Starbucks.
Many a time I challenged Him, and,
always with a short giggle

He walked away gracefully saying . . .
"Not yet . . .
Not yet . . . I
have things for you to do . . ."

My spirit I summon from the
realms of the void,
to descend in the roots and
trace a course.

I dive deep past all
sunlit gates of consciousness
looking for a sign,
straight sign like a blue spruce

with duty marked on its fresh bark.
I search for a beacon,
as the lyre slices the air
in pieces of silver.

I dive deep past all
golden gates of my roots
I summon the humble plow, and,
the path I carve

on the tired face of
mother Earth.
I plow a course towards
the light of a beacon.

Lantern

The lantern's wisdom I embrace, and,
the narrow path in front
I unfold with all good inspiration
for the discovery of the one.

        Sardonic laughs,
        ironic smiles, short,
        ever short images of stolen gazes
        when a young sun struggles

to transform the world
into golden miracles.
Human banality overcomes
all the dreams of the dreamers.

        A lantern's wisdom I present
        to my feet,
        for my feet to follow, perhaps
        this morning, perhaps today,

I'll find Him.
Perhaps this morning
I'll find the one
who sees man like a man.

Perhaps today
I'll get to meet the One
who doesn't stay at the color
of a garment, or a skin,

who doesn't esteem
the value of a bank account,
or the number of missiles
pointed against the other man.

Tired footsteps in the agora[*], and
in the arena, and
in the matador's dreams,
as I endure the ridicule of

the non existent life forms
as I endure the pain of searching
for a piece of the endless blue sky.
Tired footsteps up the steep

face of daylight and the blind
hands of the moonlight.

[*]*market*

Affirmation

I dive deep where all light reigns
roots of my ancestors, and
the pieta of cyclamens I meet,
in search for a beacon,

        the beacon, when on the love for all
        enameled images I stumble.
        «Δομήνικος Θεοτοκόπουλος, Κρής, εποία»[*]
        A man, how did he see man?

A man, a giant, how did he see man?
«Δομήνικος Θεοτοκόπουλος, Κρής, εποία»
A humble affirmation
of lineage, parents, siblings,

        of where a person comes from,
        of where such a soul originates.
        Reminder of where a woman's womb
        nurtured another splendorous sun,

another man,
where a woman's womb graced life
with the spirit of the Eternal.
«Δομήνικος Θεοτοκόπουλος, Κρής, εποία»

[*]*Created by the Cretan Domenikos Theotokopoulos.*

My quest I underscore for the one
I crave to uphold, once again.
A simple pronouncement of
where a man comes from, until

the latter moons when all universe
prides to call Him her son.
Latter sunlit days when the roots
reflect on the membrane of man's

thought, and the lining of man's
greed claims the remains, as
a moonless night encodes
once the where this man comes from.

Toledo

The contour of Tagos
defines your eastern border
beyond which lay all
the pious wheat fields

                with their holy reverence.
                Western bank caresses all
                homes and the dreams of angels.
                Humble city mother of art

yet so much richness
hidden in your heart
behind the veil of sunlight,
behind the husks of the

                un ripened corn.
                Toledo. Humble poor city,
                yet, with wide open arms you
                accept an orphan man and,

his vision, an orphan man and,
his passion, like
the vast wheat fields
welcome rain. Toledo.

What did you see in this man?
Toledo. How long had you
dreamed of a man such
as this man?

Toledo.
How long have you longed
for such a soul?
«Δομήνικος Θεοτοκόπουλος, Κρής, εποία»

A young man, a new city,
a new home, a modest little smile
on the lips of life
which unfolds towards perfection.

A Cretan's inspiration, and,
a desire for excellence,
for white dreams,
a Cretan's white dreams and

images from heavens.
Toledo. You have graced him with
a home. A base a home for
this young lonely Cretan.

One Sun

Only the sun,
so different,
overprotecting,
where you took your first

                breath.
                Only the soil,
                hard, colorful, unwrinkled.
                Earth forsaken, arduous,

ever enduring,
where you stepped first,
a child.
Only the blue sea,

                an angelic melody,
                a soothing whisper,
                forever dancing
                where you bathed at first,

a youth.
Only this vision,
inquiring,
wondering,

overpowering,
result of your Cretan glance
that special ray which summoned
your Goal.

A Cretan, a giant, a man,
perhaps you even had flesh.
Great ancestor,
perhaps you felt,

like a mortal,
fear, anger, grief.
Great ancestor,
I admire your courage.

Pilgrimage

Trembling steps, scared,
mesmerized anticipation
sweet wonderment,
steps on a pilgrimage,

>   to the holy enclave,
>   where man, a man opened
>   the gates of heaven for the eyes
>   of a hungry world.

Steps one by one upwards
a staircase upholds hope
towards the cosmos of
man, of a man, of a Giant,

>   a cosmos which still stands
>   between the quakes of the wheat
>   and the pain of the asphodels.
>   Thoughts on a pilgrimage

between doubt, fear, anxiety, and
sweet wonderment
thoughts one by one upwards
between your several agonies

to achieve the impossible, and,
your passion to fight
for your ethereal world.
My steps upwards towards

the celestial world of
my great ancestor's,
on the same path with
his Cretan glance, which

sees through the world
as the sunlight through a crystal.
His Cretan glance, which
orates to the golden wheat fields

vapors of spring,
shades of a July's waist.
Respectful steps which follow
to his zenith of accomplishment

where man simply
turns to God,
where God simply
becomes Man.

Red Carpet

Like a red carpet I lay my heart
before all the ethereal fleshless
images which you have graced
with life.

Your fiery passion for greatness
a charisma which
transcends the ephemeral,
the only means you need.

Great grandfather were men
the same in your days?
How did your Cretan glance
embrace them?

How did the Cretan sun
which you carried in your heart
shine on them?
Your ever enduring masterpieces

results of your endless inspiration
a witness to this splendorous vision,
to your celestial fervor.
A witness to your

relentless effort to unfold man's
heart like the petals
of a rose, one by one.
A witness to your

undying yearning to transcend
one by one the layers
of a man's caged substance.
Step by step on the ladder upwards.

Less flesh forward:
spirit only.

Agony

Your agony pierces
the cracked wooden base
of Earth, and hovers over
your ethereal forehead, where

        all human humdrum turns
        to celestial.
        Your agony I taste
        as I sit on the chair

you once sat.
In the chromatic aura of
the devout room I sense
your heartfelt desire for divinity.

        On the velvety canvas where
        you gave birth to all perfection
        I smell your passion.
        On the devotional palette

a witness to your fiery enthusiasm
to position man next to angels
I detect your torment.
Your desire to turn man

into the cherubic essence
of the spiritual I sense.
I feel your inspiration
your devotion and your piety

I smell in the vaporous air
of your room, in the fleshless
images on the canvas,
your passion I endure.

What an overwhelming sweet
warmth in the arms of life
like a thunderous return to
the everlasting roots of our island.

Torment

Your tormented heart sadly
stares at the unbearable human
littleness which you witness,
everyday pain

                    of the fecund rosebush,
                    everyday scar
                    for your Titanic soul which
                    embraces all frugal or grand.

Is man great on your first morning?
Is man a negligible parrot
on your late dusk?
You fight, an honorable soul,

                    you fight to grasp the equilibrium
                    between all pettiness and
                    the splendorous which
                    your ardor composes on

the ever adoring canvas.
What else is there really?
Just immortality
from the hands of the mortal.

What else is there really?
Just Death and
amorous hope
from the hands of an immortal.

Lagrimas de Pedro*

A musical note,
primordial Aum
ripples through both tympanums
of the virgin world,

> a sound, a bridge between
> chaos and order
> an invention.
> One line, three words

"Lagrimas de Pedro"
ripple through both gates
of the virgin world,
a line, a bridge between

> ego's fear and the ache of a heart.
> The movement of the brush
> waves through the air
> of sulphur and darkness

a primeval sweet disorder
a kinesis,
a rope of hope between
the graceful Death

Peter's Tears . . . The Repentant Peter

of man and his unfolding
immortality.
Left eye,
graced with just one tear

two pupils with reverence
ascend in the momentum
of a celestial warmth,
a man repenting.

Balance

Capture of a blue piece
from the vastness of the sky
to compliment the miracle
of a man, or a woman, your task, and

           the word failure doesn't exist.
           This balance between the
           ethereal images, and
           the grossness of the flesh

becomes the link which
embarks from the top
of your spirit to the tip
of your brush, and

           on display on your adoring canvas.
           The link which ties
           the depths of your soul
           to the zenith of your marvels

this equilibrium, and
your Cretan sun always
there, gifting with his rays
the movement of pathos,

the song of the nightingales,
the endlessness of your glance
to the far side of the galaxy.

Here the ephemeral becomes infinite.

Here the end turns to a starting point.

Here the gross turns to abstract.

Here the stop point becomes perpetual.

Here the ever small turns Gigantic.

Here man becomes Titan.

Here your passion becomes medium.

Here your flesh turns to spirit.

Here your spirit melts into the Godly.

Spartan Room

A Spartan room endures
the steps of a Giant.
A temperate chair upholds
the weight of your stature.

                    A passionate brush sustains
                    your infinite creativity.
                    An ecstatic hand manifests
                    one by one your symbols.

A glowing Cretan sun idolizes
your colors.
A litany of your Cretan glance captures
your everlasting marvels.

                    A poetic palette stands
                    guard of your images.
                    All tools in your hands
                    angelic instruments and

your wide open heart embraces
the ascent of your idols
to the beyond
to immortality.

Judas

Sinister smile
faint grimace
left eye immense
solitude in front, and

behind you ripple of
dark Death in your mind
your tablet, your lot
cursed destiny stars weep

dark Death in your hands, and,
all the love of cosmos
choir of the nightingales
hidden in a simple kiss.

Flock of wild doves
mourns on top of the world
traitor, a murmur,
the virgin creek whispers

word written on the crest
of the horizon, the word
echoes back in your soul
traitor, a course which

you have started in the
pupil of your left eye, and
a sinister smile is gifted to
the winds for eternity.

A post allotted to you, as
posts granted to all hyacinths.
Deeply rooted in the Earth with
a staff and a heavy heart

a young earthling: You alone
on your way to Erebus.
You place both hands on the anvil
to be shaped into a fold

by the hammering time.
Sinister smile, subtle
grimace for a job well done
I know your secret now.

I know your secret now.
My Great Father crystallized it
on your obscure smirk
on this enduring canvas.

A flock of geese on the
other crest of the sky
draw the pitiful word
traitor . . . a crimson dusk

       red blood, your solitude
       graced by a simple tear, and
       all mysticism of the olive groves
       becomes an absolution in

a world which sees
only the outside.
I salute you young soldier
your post you never left.

       I salute you young hero
       you show your courage
       as you stand there with
       your perpetual sinister smile

as the heavy chiton[*] of
the renegade weights on
your shoulders forever.
I salute you young soldier.

       Time ferments history
       the grooves on your skin
       echo of a traitor hangs over
       the flight of the lonely condor

[*]*Robe*

the laugh of all hibiscus
and the lovemaking of all apes.
Yet time ferments the images
of heroes . . . I salute you.

Time moulds history, and
all good wines red blood
your blood and the hero's
destiny written on your tablet.

Your chiton heavier than the gallant's
the echo of the word traitor, and
your sinister smile on the canvas
galvanizes a new eternity.

Disorder

Steep mountain sides suffuse
pain along with endurance
chaos in the midst
of the thirsty wheat fields

        desire at war with consciousness, and
        so many steps in front of
        your mesmerizing brush
        yet, the task remains a focus.

Chaos, war, famine, and
the mediocrity of city humdrum
endlessly dictate the worth of
man's carnal appetites, when

        the realm of order appears
        from behind all dark clouds
        a sun always yearns, and
        the cherubic wind in consonance

with all splendour this first
everlasting morning, and
every short evening, ordered
rapport, uniformity slyly comes forth

an orderly nascent heaven
the heavenly order with
which you fashion your
ethereal structures.

Somehow your world, and
ours make sense.
Somehow your creation, and
our lives make sense.

Is it because of its base? Or,
is it because of its celestial foundation?
Is it because of your vision? Or,
is it because of the Cretan sun?

Jealousy, envy, chaos,
hunger, misery, littleness.
Steep mountain sides erected
in front of your vision.

Yet your ardour and energy
overcomes all obstacles
great fuser of life, what
can ever stop you.

The dew of the evening, or,
the hoarfrost of morning
life's transience, or man's
unending temporal thirst?

        Insatiable grief smiles
        through all anguish, and
        your fervour, undying eagerness
        to galvanize immortality

in the fleshless bodies of
your models, elongated figures
of men, of women, already in
their movement to the heavenly.

        Somehow, now, your world, and
        ours makes sense.
        Somehow now, these images, and
        ours make sense.

(Detail)

Laocoon

How many strands of your brush
opened the wound of chartreuse
which turns in space like the
hand of Laocoon who lifts

        one arc of an eyebrow and the veil
        of futility over the dreams of
        all dreamers. Futility in the arms
        of the flesh and the clouded images

of all idealists, all refined splendor.
Futility in the effort of the lonely
falcon to grasp in a flash of light
the heart of a tender whisper or

        the meaning of a riddle, Oedipus
        on his way to the first killing.
        The strand stands there in front
        of your brush with its goal to

create endlessness when the
mask of futility decorates a spring.
It stands there in front of the observing
graces who condone all misfortune.

Futility your weapon on the tip
of your brush which epitomizes
all engraved manifestations with
the dark shroud over their

wounds, over all whip marks.
Futility in the virgin hour of
lovemaking and in the graceful
dance of all enamored pelicans.

The ephemeral fight between
flesh and unforgiving fate
a matter for your angry brush
to capture. The developing spirit

and your pathos for opulence
summons the last hope as
by a thread and places it
in the midst of human misery

as a beacon for all the lost souls
when the blue bay at the turn
of the river which embraces
your holy city collapses.

Futility, agony and despair reign
when the only heavens you
present to this life stands as a
simple movement of the observer's

> hand which cuts the air in
> two luminous pieces.
> Your spirit and your hero
> in a desperate acceptance of all

expected and unexpected gifts.
Futility written on the garment
of the cosmos which falls open
flows and trails always

> upwards. Then the tip of your
> brush wicks the light up
> to the lonely strand of an
> eyebrow which describes

the pain of a heart forever.
Pain which eulogizes the fight
of all life forms in the arms of
the most futile and enduring hope.

Thorny Crown

A thorny crown beautifies
the ever benevolent head and
trees in meditation, some red
stigmata and your devotion

          a voracious hunger. Your suffering
          when you only see a mission,
          the only mission of transcending
          all smallness of man.

The man of your era and
ours, great teacher, all
tiny-mindedness of man of
every era

          with the power of light
          which you cherish in your heart.
          The power of light which
          always leads your vision.

A vision the Cretan sun
has bestowed on you.
Your Cretan sun and the foresight
of your Cretan wisdom

which sees through a man
as the sun sparkles through a diamond.
The birth of fragrant rose
from your stimulating brush

and the figures with transparent
angular intensity orate
words of understanding
to the moments, to eternity.

Cherubs

Your eyes get immersed in the aura
of a Cretan sun, and your masterpieces
not semblances of men, or,
of women, just reflections

        of angels in a mirror.
        Just idols of cherubs,
        archangels and seraphs with
        wings which open and close

like a mysterious fan
in front of the splendor
of a sublime likeness, and
a stalactite of your love

        descends to moisten all
        dryness, to quench all thirst.
        Your love, oh, great Cretan, for
        man, for life, for God.

Here the line between
the spirit and flesh becomes
so indistinguishable
so tragically vague.

Here the aura of God
and the shadow of man
fuse into a ripple of gray air
into the sadness of a beacon.

These tears freely cascade
and overwhelm the afternoon heat
love songs heard of before
these tears become the absolution

of a thunderous encounter
between a Giant and a man
who has dared Death many a time,
man who cares to reach higher.

Caged Spirit

Deep cisterns of tears and
caged spirit when a plow dives
in the flesh of the earth
lamentation and vapors of dreams

permanence captive
loss of a bird's game
eternal joy in the prison
of an undulating Death

then all of a sudden
the borderline erases itself
like a lonely falcon in a
wall of immense fog

is flesh the orphan or
the spirit a murmur on the free wind?
Your mind captures in a flash
this moment of synthesis, and

seized by a stroke, by a fine
contour, by a line, a fused aura
the ever accepting canvas
presents to anticipation.

Your patient canvas which
compliments all effort
dedication of golden arms
in the sunset of a dream.

Canvas like a child in
a class with hands folded
as the miracle defines itself
almost and the essence

of reality lies exposed
forever.

Antithesis

Impeccable clarity the soil
from the sky's transparency
where all others see
endless muddy fears, and

                    the volcano stares at the
                    sun, a passion traces bids
                    of blood, air split in bronze
                    palaces, mazes and Death.

Vision of where man goes
the wealth of images, and
the fervor of which life
the desolate canyon echoes

                    angelic splendor, radiance
                    where all others see
                    monstrous fleshy imprisonment
                    your inquiry for the features

of God in the semblances
of your ascending marvels.
Your consummation of how
God emanates in the form of human.

Unswerving dedication,
steadfastness, when the weak
stop at the first gate, your
pilgrimage to the altar of

the spirit, a tantalizing
endeavor for the completion
of the immortal task: One
spirit only . . . Just one.

Unity

The single stroke of a chord
unleashes an undressed note
which reverberates through
the laughing air, and

a sound dangles a free flow.
A quixotic fantasy and an eclectic
guise unfolds, the eagle's
talons there under unwrapped

two strokes of your magic brush
relentlessly accentuate
a splash of red, and
a half hidden shade of black.

Mixture of murmur
and silence manifests
the invincible endurance
of a man's task in front

of a line, a few words,
an unbearable stanza
which persistently insists in
defying time, as always.

A stanza persistently insists in
defying Death: This is the course
to immortality. Oh, great ancestor,
what else is there to yearn for?

A single note dangling
two strokes of a brush accentuating
a stanza persistently defying Death
the only path to defeat transience.

Reverence

Reverence for the tears
of the cyclamens and
the assonance between all
images and the shadow of fear.

Reverence for the refined
face and the bloated ego
of all foolish. Reverence for the cistern
of woes and the oar less raft

which carries banality.
Reverence for the splendor
of the spirit permanently
engraved on your canvas

on every canvas,
on all the canvasses of the cosmos.
Yet light in constant fight
against the cheap Lucifer

a war against a cheat,
the market scoundrel
who cares for his daily take
this man's life, this man's peace.

Reverence for the fervor
of your brush which graces all images
with the rhythm of passion, and
the agony of your love.

El Entierro del Señor de Orgaz*

It withers in time, an oak
ravaged by wind and stone
by the light or perhaps by
Erebus, an oak withers, and

> the flesh of man.
> Nothing abides but silence
> when the foresight of a genius
> like a plow unearthing a course

a master with the Cretan sun
with the Cretan glance
solitaire beacon
desolate visionary

> chisels the images on a
> canvas and a soft shoulder
> for the crying falcons
> a nascent masterpiece.

The threefold essence of the count
like all others reflects in
the eyes of all auroras.
The aura stands on foot

*The burial of the count of Orgaz

solid grasp of the ground.
The flesh captivates the depths
of the grave and the spirit
ascends to the heavens.

One man withers in time
an oak ravaged by the
banality of city life, and
insatiable carnal pleasures.

The burial of the count Orgaz
fusion of the present with the after
passage through this door
a curtain unfolds like a flower

the symmetric parade of geese
which vex the horizon like angels
on their way to fetch a soul
the instant metamorphosis

of the carnal to the ethereal
in the hands of a master
life transcends with just
one magic stroke, and

the mortal becomes eternal.
One essence compliments
the tear enhanced seclusion
duality in transition, endlessness.

New World

Here I enter the world
of an immortal as the trees
on the other side of the river
meditate their good fortune.

A slight shiver through my spine
as your wonders smile and
the chair you once sat in laments
as the ruffle of the air

sings of your Death to the
lonely hawk and to the pious
peasant. You put your hand
on the anvil once again and

a sweet babble overtakes
my heart. Water in the river
sleeps for a while as the realm
of the spirit opens like a rose and

rudimentary sound of order
hovers in a young, blue
universe which you create
with your ambitious brush.

In the realm of nascent pathos
where does the line mark
my flesh, your flesh, Great Father?
Your celestial new world appears as

a humble resonance which echoes
to the ends of space and
in the tympanums of the dreams.
The night weeps in the fairytales

of the laughing children and
it all makes sense now, yes,
in the eyes of your Cretan sun
there is no ephemeral light.

Just immortal and your hand
as in a miracle guides your
brush to unfold reality like
the joyous heart of a child.

It all makes sense now
deathless chromatism,
splendorous fusion of ethereal
with the invincible earthly

define your immortality.
The marvels on these canvasses
speak in a celestial tongue
of your agony to display them

        for the blue young world to see.
        It all makes sense now, and
        this smooth shiver in my spine
        turns to a sweet warmth.

There is no flesh anymore
just a choir of nightingales.
There is no Death left
but the harmony of your harp.

Brush

Exhausted auroras and the flower
stems injure the love song of
the night. The people's golden ears
shiver and your brush a busy bee

           takes all life underarm
           and graces it with
           immortality.
           The brush which delightfully

kills all temporal.
The brush in the fingers
of a man who is guided
by the unending creativity and

           an angelic vision grants
           all images with an ethereal
           accentuation of invincible life.
           The brush galvanizes all

subterranean impulses
on a canvas and transcends
all primeval wants into
fleshless seraphic configurations

which suddenly appear
like mutant stars with a sign
on their forehead which compliments
the tear enriched solitude.

Solitude reveals for the first time
the great vision of a Cretan
who shines like an apparition in
the crystal curve of the sky.

Hesitation

Your hand hesitates on its way
to inscribe the orphan's dream.
It wonders what to do,
how to engrave the tear

        of the widow's pain and
        the black symbol of her garment
        how to idolize transience, as
        nothing remains but solitude.

Then a single sunray intervenes
from the realm of the smiles.
From the orphans' smiles and
from the widows' laugh

        where a sunray dances every short April
        and every long October.
        The master's hand captures
        this eternal laugh and

his brush immortalizes
this forbearing smile.
It all makes sense now
in his world and in ours.

Where there was chaos
there is now order.
Where there was pain
there is now laughter.

Where there was flesh
there is now spirit.
Where there was Death
there is now immortality.

Leaden Cloud

An inert cloud
suffuses on the canvas and
blankets the golden waves
of the wheat fields.

> The spine of the lonely
> rooster squirms and
> the poets' pen freezes.
> The palette rejects all colors

and time laments as it conquers
the condor's talons.
Leaden cloud: An image:
Death ever invincible: An apparition,

> victorious platinum vestment
> for a vain life
> short breath and
> a master ascents

to grant light: Once.
A visionary appears
with his colourful palette and
like playful child in a schoolyard

with his brush which
knows grace he gifts with
just two strokes the image
of immortality to the world.

Echo

Profound resonance
stark echo of the
chickadee's flutter
in front and

        your brush rises and
        captures in a flash of light
        the meaning of permanence
        opposing the slow Death

of everyday life
in a city, or, a prison,
in the battle ground
or the dark underworld.

        Profound resonance
        on the chamomiles and
        the thunderous sound of
        primordial beginnings

where the echo of your pathos
galvanizes time and
in an infinitesimal fraction
of a life, or a breath

it defines the borders of a goal
from the humdrum of
the avarice enclave
of money or shallow fame.

Absence

Images of ethereal bodies
inscribe a path and
where is man?
The oar less raft floats

          against all misery and
          Poseidon's anger.
          Layer of accomplishment
          the celestial figures and

where is man?
The rudderless raft drifts
in the midst of a tempest when
his dreams somehow

          turn ugly.
          Tantalizing thought of a man
          enriched with littleness
          bloated with pettiness and

Death.
When you gift him with
your vision, when
you grace him with

the immortality of your hands
the love of your heart
when you gift him with
your passion and clarity

of vision, when you beautify him
with eternal light, where is man?
When you stand to embrace him
with open arms

where is man?
No one comes.
Where is man?
No one comes.

El Espolio*

Iridescent eyes and transparency
which eludes the cosmic
morph the outer world in colors
and enamelled images.

        The crystallized ethereal
        interior life and
        ambition guides
        the steps of the lion.

The red carnage
the husk of the ripened corn and
the sap of the tree still
command the mesmerized

        molecules to march ahead.
        They adorn this translucent
        essence which in just two strokes
        of the compliant brush of the master

transforms the life of a saint.
With a newfound breath
they move it further higher
than all angels, far

*The Spoliation–The Disrobing

deeper than any meaning.
Iridescence fathomed apparitions
of a man reaching higher
as the hordes of the wolves

howl from the thicket
close by, the wolves just
in a contour of Death.
The prey, a red carnage

in the outer world of
dominance and the shine
of the master's Cretan sun
salutes immortality.

Palette

The fusion of all streams
towards the big father on
the way to the ocean, this
palette's unlimited pathos.

           Mixture of colors
           chromatic paradise
           your brush a medium
           between vision and miracle.

Strokes underscore
all refined contours
intensify the love
of the jasmines, and

           vague chromatism affirms
           the Eros of all orchids, and
           the splendorous beyond.
           Furthermore than man's ambition

the master's play ground.
Plain words, simple symbols
humble intention to
outline the greatness of your spirit

and identify with one's origin
one's link to transcendental.
Palette's unlimited pathos
with the master's celestial roots.

Ambivalence

The light enamours
your forehead and
all this warmth blankets
my heart,

        caresses my eyes. Your
        mission fuses with the well being
        of life and exposes itself
        to the forked ambivalence.

You walked next to me
by the hill side that Eastern
afternoon when we gathered
the wild saffron, when

        we talked to the
        fragrant oregano…
        The Cretan Sun overhead spread
        its golden arms in the sunset.

Sweet warmth in this room
where you captured eternity
with just a simple stroke
of your beloved brush.

It all makes sense now,
oh, great ancestor,
just one stroke is needed,
always, just one line,

just one note and
the temporal transcends
as the myth of creation
vexes the myth of light.

Fusion

One stroke and light
one stanza and light
one note and light.
Your breath a stroke on the canvas

          and your hand evokes the miracle.
          Your heart enamors all spirits.
          Your love for man
          galvanizes time.

Light in your images
light in this stanza
light in your song.
One sun under the Cretan sky

          and one sun where you took
          your first breath aroma
          which graces the butterflies.
          One sun under the Cretan sky

where we walked towards
the lonely cenotaph on the hillside.
One sun where we danced
the pentozalis* in the crimson dawn.

*Graceful folk dance

Two hearts on a path of duty
always thorns and pain.
One essence accentuating
the miracle of creativity

which redefines the word commitment
and reveals the strong desire of
your vision and your passion for
the ever splendorous creation.

Exaltation

A Cretan on the narrow path
body in the entrapment
of flesh and of a vision,
a blue dawn and a black horse

        with Hades riding the clouds.
        My grant father on the narrow path
        with the stamina of an old body and
        a vision for the eternal, voices

which torment the dreams
of all dreamers, of all inspired poets.
A line serves as a bridge
over the gap of two auras and

        the secret of the wind's murmur.
        A Cretan walks together with faith
        and the sun above never leaves.
        The humble manger where

you first smiled at the
warmth of the sunrays
before the orchids fermented
the usual sensuality and a trip

you took to the far away Toledo.
A course on the face of Earth
ploughed by your desire for
endless knowledge and a passion

which formulated the eternal
in the shape of the human.
The eternal in the shape of a man
in a unified tautology.

Ascension

Golden petals of your heart
open wide and become
shelter and refuse for all small
and weak as the last aurora

        still sings the celestial song of
        creativity and the tip of your brush
        with a simple wave chisels
        your ascension as nothing here

can keep you from the eternal.
The angel from above smiles
as your spirit shows the way
to him and to all lost souls.

        The direction only upwards
        like all your marvels which already
        take such a liberating walk
        in your celestial masterpieces, oh great

father, nothing else matters
when a man comes to this
point of fusion with the ever
splendorous and deathless.

Nothing else matters, oh
great father, when the last song
still murmurs your ascension
and the last chickadee rejoices

the primeval song of all
golden harps, the last colourful
cloud draws a breath from the
blue leaves of the sky.

The colourful cloud draws a breath
from the blue leaves of the sky
and you look at the mirage downwards
as you simply become spirit.

Μανώλης, Κρής, εποία

About the Author

Manolis was born in the island of Crete in 1947. He was educated in Greece at thePanteios Supreme School of Athens: BA in Political Sciences and he served in the armed forces for two years, then emigrated to Vancouver, Canada in 1973. He attended Simon Fraser University for a year, taking English literature in a non-degree program and he has written three novels and a number of collections of poetry (which are slowly appearing as published works), various articles and short stories, in Greek as well as in English.

After working as an iron worker, a train laborer, a taxi driver and a stockbroker, Manolis retired in 1998. Now he lives in White Rock and he spends his time writing, gardening, and traveling.